i like you
like you

i like you
like you
poems
by
Lancee Whetman

Visit the author's website at www.vigilancee.org

ISBN: 979-8-9897302-3-0

Table of Contents

n. the mental state of being madly in love or intensely infatuated when reciprocation of the feeling is uncertain

What if liking is its own kind of love?

I LIKE YOU, LIKE YOU

Tomorrow,
I want to touch you
like I did last week—
under-the-table hands.

I don't want to grapple
with the ineffable.

I don't want to wick away
like candle wax.

I want to remember
how cherry stems taste
when they aren't
knotted up
in your mouth.

What do your words taste
like?

Is it like an
I love you?

Or an *I like you, like you*
like *that*?

FROM HIS PERSPECTIVE

too slow for actual speed / movement of tongues / heals the separation / hardware / hard / wired / for a panel of familiar vices / and gargantuan closeness / monster of cheekiness / advise our future selves / to repeat the same act / truck footsie / footloose / the notion that we're fireworks / just friends / explosive in the ether / in the trenches / of available tempos / the aftermath of a four-year wait / the injection of the rowdy quiet / acid trip at 24 / tell her I love her / (kind of) / by making breakfast / and making her / mine

TWINED

Remember us?
Peas-in-a-pod people?
Emulating the swans and all their
to
get
her
ness?
Sometimes, it can feel brackish
to bind.
But what the heck, let it.

Hold tight.

The tides bring in the best
treasure.

Return us to our place
hands intertwined
in the spectacular normal.

EXPERIMENT KITCHEN

I want to write about how self-conscious I am
when cooking for others—
how, to learn, I devoured pages
of *Cook's Illustrated.*

How I started with Gà Kho Gừng
because it was the only dish
I already had the ingredients for.

How I deboned the chicken
kept some skin, some plump pockets of fat.
How I sliced ginger into matchsticks
how pungent shallots stung my eyes
how garlic fumed into my nostrils.

How sugar—white, crystalline—
met oil and heat
turned from pale to honey
to the deep sheen of soy sauce.
I watched the breakdown
of fructose and glucose
called my lab: *Experiment Kitchen.*

How fish sauce and coconut milk
made my mouth water before the first bite
a hunger born of science and instinct.
After abiding by the laws of cooking timers
I spooned up a taste test.
The so-called umami flavor
(more like *ooh-yummy* flavor)
was there.

I served dinner.
Told my partner: *Eat.*
Knowing full well
this would be the first time
he would want
seconds.

THE CAPE

Washing-machine white waves—
the crest of an incoming tide.
Wind gusts.

Sand-drift central.
Our legs lurching up dunes
running starts, critical momentum.

A hand reached out
to lift me over mounds—
not molehills.

We wandered—
exploratory outings.

Though I am long-legged
you walk faster.
My pace and pulse
quicken to keep up—
body warm with the effort.

In search of what the sea surrendered,
you always find the finest beach treasures.

No competition
but if it were—
you'd win.

Today: a fossil
of vertebrae
an ancient fragment.

Before we left the Cape
you placed a sand dollar in my palm—
so simple
yet the moment
became so much more.

When the bellowing coastal air
called us back
by bush plane
you prepped the flight—

taxiing, takeoff
landing—
the sky's crosshairs can be tricky.

But I know
this—us—
isn't.

THIRTEEN YEARS RIPER

My partner is thirteen years riper than I—
which is to say, *older*
in the sense of the human-made concept of time.

After a certain point
we stop ascertaining age differences.
Love doesn't abide
by trips-around-the-sun calculations.

We breathe the same lungfuls of life.
Every exchange between us—energistic.

We're in different phases of body accounting.
His brown hair: salt-streaked
enough to notice.
I haven't found any yet.

He calls me *foxy*.
I am his biggest silver-fox fan.

In the morning
as we part from the bed sheets
his aches linger longer than mine.
We note it, nonchalantly
side by side on yoga mats.

We take our tea
with a side of mobility.

My hands find knots in his calves
like oiling a well-running machine-man.

Evenings come slow.
We walk the tundra—
its bubbly surface demanding balance:
ligament, knee, ankle.

We're grateful to walk this road
knowing thirty years from now
might offer a different answer.

We don't admit we've passed our apogee
that our bodies will become earthen ash
once the soul has finished its lease.

But our bodies are only a piece of this life.

Inside
we haven't wilted.

Outside,
we are still capable of so much.

We still banter about who takes
longer in the bathroom.
We still consume *Infinite Jest* like it's hard candy.
We still make choices.

And death?
We don't deny it.
We just don't invite it in.

We share Christmas with our families
listen to new music on the jukebox.
Stay up late enough to catch
a few more midnights.

We monopolize on the mundane—

former misfits
who once worried about
all the wrong things.

Now
we cherish the blush of grace
the soft embarrassment
of letting ourselves be seen.

We finish each other's sentences.
When I say I...
He says *love you.*

He pours the coffee.
We sit on the front porch swing.
We are gracious with our sunwrinkles
our silhouette dances.

It's all uncertain.
It always has been.

Age?
It just doesn't know
which one of us
it will take
first.

FOREVERS

In
the
end
there will be effervescence
and eternity

perhaps emerald
and other detonations
of forever.

Circles around our fingers
reminders of infinity
that replays

like Sunday

like bedsheets

like time-warp sex.

FIRST TIME MEETING IN PERSON

I have too much to
say. Not enough time to say
I like you, like you.

THE NEW GIRL

The new girl in town
is tall, beautiful—
olive-oil skin
silky brunette hair.

She just finished knitting
two wool sweaters
for winter.
She looks regal
even while berry-picking
in a blizzard
of bird-sized mosquitoes.

She grew up in the Bahamas
until she was twelve.
Knows how to spear
and slingshot fish
for dinner.

She studied environmental journalism—
wants to save the planet
with her words.

She's gentle
soft-spoken.
Laughs the kind of laugh
you hope is meant
for your jokes.

She has a cat.
Lives beachfront.
She got the million-dollar-view
apartment I was denied—
because I had a puppy.

The new girl in town
looks like the type of girl
(and is the type of girl)
my boyfriend would like

and maybe

me too.

MUSICALITY

If we were chords
you: 43
a playful major.
Me: 29
a somber minor.

Note:
my breaths
around you
always
measure in eighths.

CORN-MAZE SEASON

I guess you can flirt
with formaldehyde
'til you're coffin-dead—
demanding a funeral
fuck.

Red turtleneck revelry—
matching the leaves
then left
like a nuded branch.

Reaching out like a gourd
a glitch
a glamorous costume.

I am pumpkin-spice bait.
Dancing through decaying decor—
Earth-confetti.

Catching scold-like feelings
falling faint
at full moons
hacking down a howl
like I'm *bitch*.

Gyrating hips
give me goosebumps.
Lover's rump—
roll
like it's hallowed.
A reverent haunting
a chance to lose ourselves.

Call this:
corn-maze season.

Come.
Make my cunt
a cauldron.

SHE'S FROM SALT LAKE CITY, UTAH

Men, girls, non-binary dreams—
variety is life's real spice.
And this poem?
Anything but vanilla.

Lancee's Recipe:
bisexual basil,
orgasmic oregano.
Skip the polyamorous paprika—
a dash of minty monogamy will do
for now.

Rail-me rhubarb.
Cum-again cumin.
Cuddle-me cinnamon.
Waiting for the moment he NUT—
megs.
Clitoral cilantro.
Ginger touches.
Rosemary-red cheeks.
Bay-leaf bae.

Don't slice her tenderloin heart
too deep—
but if you do, make it sting.
Like her birthplace
just add salt.

THE WEEK IS A BASKETCASE

My jaw—
a timetable.
Clockwork love.
Tissues take a seat—
tears on hiatus.
I surrender to bouquets—
no longer
a red-rose rebel.

The movies reinforce
hand-holding techniques
and soft skin multipliers.
Divide me
by bold tactics.
Am I exempt
from reaching without revelation?

Dare our orbits
to collide.
Are we pulling
the heart before the horse?

Eavesdrop
on my pulse.
Tell it to beat—
drummer fast.
Symbols.
Applause for going steady.
The pillows want an encore.

Swallow my lungs
so I can breathe
your same vicinity.

TO BE SMART

On our FaceTime date, Doug asks, hypothetically:
If two people walked by you—one who knew you, one who didn't—and the one who didn't asked, 'Who is that?' How would you want the person who knew you to describe you?

I think for a moment, then answer: *Endearing.*

I ask how he would describe me. He says: *A hoot.*

I turn the question back on him. He pauses, then says that, for the longest time, he wanted people to say he was *smart*. I believe it. Everything about him—his posture, his perfect punctuation, his glasses—suggests someone who has always been defined by intellect. But based on observation, it seems like that want is fading.

I told him what I thought his modus operandi was: cross-country skier, runner, highly educated. He deflects when I mention that cross-country kids are statistically the smartest in their school. Eventually, he admits he was top of his class. A test-taking machine.

He is the opposite of me in so many ways.
I have never been a great standardized test taker.
He wears his varsity calculus sweater like a medal. I failed AP Calculus.

But Doug, although extremely smart, never treated me like I wasn't—never reduced me to my LSAT or bar exam score. He saw me for who I am, because of my personality, not in spite of it.

I can't help but think about all the men who never took me seriously for being endearing—how much harder I've had to work because I didn't get the "optimal score" on an exam.

How I argued a novel legal theory against the highest-ranked male student in my law school. How my professor told me I was one of the best researchers she ever had—only for that same (male) student to turn to me and say: *If it's so good, how come they didn't argue that at the Supreme Court?*

A male friend once admitted to me: *I didn't take you seriously at first.*

Maybe that's why I believe I am endearing—because I refuse to harden, no matter how much the world tries to shape me otherwise.

Maybe that's what happens when you've made it out of the worst of your depression—you start noticing all the good again. The minutiae of every moment. How the fridge makes the same whirring sound at 2 a.m. How Howdy looks at me like I need a walk more than she does.

Maybe I am too much of a poet. Too much of a margins-scribbler. Too much of a lover, a daydreamer, a head-in-the-clouds idealist.

Maybe I flinch at the sight of commitment.

Maybe I take too many long afternoon naps.

Maybe I can't compute fast, even with a calculator.

Maybe I don't know how to be in a relationship for more than a year.

Maybe I don't know the first thing about finance, or proving self-defense in a court of law, or why the Supreme Court always seems to say: *We need not address this issue.*

But I can trust my gut like it's tarot. I can be curious about the world and wake up each day—all giddy and wanting—wondering about this Blue Dot from a new angle.

I can, if he is willing, teach Doug how to write a love poem and have him believe it's good enough.

And maybe, for once, I want the person passing me, who knows me, to turn to the other person who doesn't know me and say:

She's smart, too.

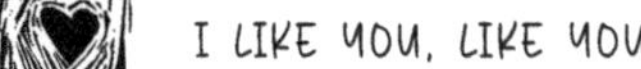

FEMALE COP

I looked into her eyes
and I was arrested.

VERSES I'D ONLY SEND VIA SNAPCHAT

Ten seconds (or less) to see it. It's a one-click *I love you*. Because if it's said on Snapchat, it feels more secure. Safer to be temporal, clicking to be casual. To be confident is to send a text, which can be archived, copied, resent, and therefore, regretted. The *I love you* came after a bottle of pinot grigio.

First, a picture of the bottle's empty contents. Send.

Second, a picture of me. Text included: *ILY* (short for you know what). Send.

Contemplate the chardonnay next. Drink.

Then realize the Snap went unopened for an hour.

Then two.

Now it's midnight, and I'm in a wine-drunk dizzy fit. *I love you* is a three-word poem that I now wish would disappear.

Against rationality, I send a third and, pray-to-God, final Snap.
Fourth. A *jk. Lol.*

I want to vanish.

It now makes sense why Snapchat's symbol is a ghost.

DINNER DATE AT NORTHRUP PLACE

Slice the evening, on bias—
a 45-degree disarming.
Make it spicy: discerningly
reckless. A bit naïve
like an MTV *Cribs* greeting.

Is that sidewalk chivalry
or just sectional theory?
Couch the conversation
in Westchester Lagoon
Chester Creek
Chuck E. Cheese Chester
childhood trauma.

Pick the bottle of riesling
that is the most "poetic."
I'd give him
all the decorative yellow
sunflowers,
tell him he's
in gold-star territory.

Learn the sonic quality
of a roaring wood stove—
a blush, a bouquet
a left-ear piercing.
So piercing.
All I want to ask is:
What's up?
And for him to say,
Northrup.

FLIGHT PATH

Old Blue and you
take me to new heights
(and to the coast). We fly
above crashing waves.
Bird's-eye view. The bay
of herring milt—
now that's what I call an orgy,
you say.

Beach-combing for hours:
two gallons of washed-ashore
R&R whiskey.
I collect sea shells
but don't sell them
by the seashore.
You identify each skeletal remnant—
whale vertebrae
shark egg sack
cod.

Looking out to Round Island
you held my hand
as we joked about
the "densely" populated beach
of just us.

On the flight path back
we saw
a bald-eagle specter
the prance of a wolf
a stalky moose
sow and cubs
caribou.
What didn't we see
that all-around Alaskan day?
I say: *This can't get any better.*

For dinner
you grilled teriyaki ribs
changed the oil in my Toyota
called me your *girl*
which landed somewhere
in between it all.

SUPERBOWL

I must note:
I don't know anything about music.
or whatever major thing
is happening in the world of sports.
I don't know which fragrance suits me—
just body-odor nerves.

Why did I fumble
an *I love you*
lodged in the barbequed
enameled crevices
only floss can reach?
Where the pigskin kisses
the 100-yard line?
This pigs-in-a-blanket mouth.

Quarterback.
Score.
It's a scandal
to yearn for yards
you.

A gamble
to hope for goals.
Guesswork, really.

It takes serious labor
just to be a fool.
Rush forward.
Fullback
or pulling back?

Why do sloppy joes
and jalapeño poppers
give me this celebration belly?

Why am I so afflicted
by underdogs—
and your undergarments?

NAUGHTY LIST

Clandestine Christmas.
Coveted affairs.
He went down
South-Pole style.
Red-stocking footsie.
Mistletoe misbehavin'.
What is lust but something seasonal?

IF LOVING YOU HAD WARNING LABELS

I wouldn't read the disclaimers. The bold lettering. The *do not do this without supervision*. The detailed side-effect list. The toxic dosage that touches my lips. The ingredients that would eventually poison each atria. I would let each chambered beat absorb a kiss. Why is there a temptation to always overdo it? An accelerated pulse is the addiction. The panic is just placebo. I would. I just know it. I would breathe in the secondhand smoke; the cologne regret. I would. I swear it. I know the fumes aren't foolproof; but they're intoxicating. Lungs are the first to fail before the next Marlboro. It was my first, you handing me your last, lighting it, telling me: *It'll cut the edge. I promise.*

OFFICIATE THE FIRST MESSAGE

I will have and hold
every insecure preamble
of your beginner poem—*It's the Good Grief*
we feel.
Love's gotten
a little expensive lately
so make me chortle a yodel
over text—
and make me your next
brains-and-buttons
neuroscientist experiment.

Maybe I am just some iteration
of Mary Oliver
an unHinged manic-pixie-dream girl.
Hey, I can't blame you
for hes-
itating.
I say: *I'm selling all my stuff.*
Next stop: Seattle.
No sleep there (I hear).
Just spontaneity.

To hell with it all.
I ask: *Wanna grab a drink?*
(Even though I don't really
drink anymore).
The Local Tide is pulling
me back, baby—
Alaska bid me *adieu.*
Time to let Saturn
return me
to the next map-dot stop.

Mr. Mason, it's nice to know
you're a believer-in-the-magic.
Maybe Spotify-divulging
does us both some good.
It ought to.
We deserve the simulation
to go right
just once
(maybe twice).
At least for a refrain, perhaps?

So play the question game for the nth time
(and like it).
Is your dog named after
Walt or Sam Whitman?
Did you know my last name's
Whetman?
What are the odds?

Tell me the boats
the light
the planets
and the chemistry in our heads
are always changing.
So fuck it all and fall
in love with it.

I say *Howdy*
as an introduction.
Realize I've gone
more West than
upstate New York.
Wonder if you've got swag
or New England slang still.
Say *forget about it*
like *fuhgeddaboudit.*

Just forget about it,
I say,
after sending you
this poem.

ORGANIC

Increase my heart rate
with a vegan kiss—
clean-bill-of-health sex.
Pesticide-free fuck.
Free-range orgasm.
Outstretch my tongue;
limerence tastebud.

SITUATIONSHIPS WANT

something
short-term
in Seattle.

sure, you say *hi*
which turns into a hug
turns into haggling
to take another Dirty Harry's
hike together.

adapt, we say
this thing we do
in the interim.
we're in each other's
shoulder
season.

when the time comes
say *goodbye*
with an unequivocal end.
it's a radical sensation.
final
as wind
as gemini
as millennial slang
as me.

let's remember Pearl
the white whale
sprinter van.
the way I got to experience
my first tank-top summer
after four years up North.
no mosquitos
just a buzz after one IPA.

let me turn 30.
tell me *that* was the best
year you haven't reached yet.
call me *sugar mama*
(even though you always paid).

DOWN BAD

with possibility / signal in the rain's momentum / regurgitate the storm warning / sight the target / but miss all three wishes / for a temporary reprieve / let's interweave / go all wicker-basket / crack jokes at all the chauvinists / then dance ourselves silly / be prey to your decent exposures / captivate the fire alarms / soak in all the nostalgia / I say / I've been looking for some hay / in all the needle stacks / unsure of the current / timetable / circumstances / is it Monday / Tuesday / all I know is / I'm beaming /

WASHED CLEAN

Rile ourselves up—riverside.
Outpouring breath
imbalance of lung
riptide exhalation.
Wim Hof theory.

We stutter, confronted
by a salmonberry rush.
Towel trustee—hold it up
while I undress:
bottoms, bare
as you drop it.

Take me from behind
and back in—
an innocent detour.
Drown in Monday's urgency.

Grab our evergreen attire.
Lost glasses—
lenses and senses slipping.
We are all doggone dry
then doggone wet.
Stream. Lake.
A poem's liquidity
dripping
down our tongues
and lips.

AUTOMATIC

Cheek aflame.
Riesling blush.

Fuck me
(almost) on the futon.

Convex on second
base.

Prayer candle.
Genuflect.

Reflect a kiss.
Deflect the sex.

Period.

Refrigerator back
chilled intensity.

Break the glass
(on accident).

Whip it out
the vacuum

I mean.
It's the first time

something else
sucks.

LOWMAN BEACH

Skipping stones
down at Lowman Beach.
Was the summer already gone
or just out of reach?

When you behold
the last day of June
does it ring out
like the Pacific's gentle tune?

Remember back
to when rocks touched feet.
Simple nights
eating farmer's market strawberries.

Oh darling, can you hear my voice
in the Puget Sound?
Are you going to miss me
when July rolls around?

It takes some will
to take that first plunge—
the way the sun dips, like lips
as they lunge.

When the truck is packed
and goodbye stands near
embarking out
is the mistress she held dear.

Will you remember the way
we hiked in our Sunday best?
How you practiced knots
on my wrists
and called it *midnight's arrest.*

KIWI

She slurps up
the tart seeds.

Wipes her face
on the napkin.

I am her
favorite
fruit.

READING SMUT

I don't usher in illumination / but I understand the provocativeness of lightbulb ideas / only when there is sky / high as sympathetic gravity / there is never enough literature to underline / to finalize the bloodstream / to iron out the oxygen / in our vein vernacular / I took from treasure chests / but only as an adult / I am secondary espionage / seam-ripper indecisive / I made him question his suave nature / haircut season / stair-stepper shave / don't leave subtly / only with a prickle-kiss / the last remnant / coin-flip the scissors / manipulate my lip / fold romance into the module / the making of the bed / and the ruin we made of it.

CROSS-STAR CIRCUITRY

Zoom into the ethereal
soundscape—
a Gregorian chant overture.

The microphotographic universe
of irises.
Sand-grain time.

Capture twigged outliers,
outcroppings of beach—
a divine harvest
of cedar and cloud.

Macro senses:
touch the brocaded sunlight.
It is as pragmatic
as ultraviolet poison
stripping us of our shirts.

We walk into the water—
for lechery, for love,
to integrate circuits.

Wires crossed
just like the stars.

SPICY

Hot Italian
sausage. Dinner innuen-
do. No leftovers.

KATIE

In English
they say *chemistry*.

But in French
it is *la chimie*.

Chicago culled us
together like a Woodwind martini
like St. James cathedral
like the catharsis of an
Episcopal eternity.

Brilliance is not just business.
It is the beauty
in the beholding;
in the Midwest

that makes
us winding
wanting
all
tornado

wild.

FIELD NOTES FROM THE PENINSULA

A *Lord of the Rings* stick
aids our side quest
into the Pacific—
barnacle toes.

You mack on me
after an orca sighting.
Black-and-white lottery.
Pod closeness.
Beach squirts.

Nap Time: Part One.

Date idea:
bald-eagle viewing
and poo harvesting
our respective dogs' shit.

Nap Time: Part Two.

Buy a Walmart skort for summer.

Swish of wind on bare leg.

Down a Fisherman's Friend—
sore throat
foggy outlooks.

We hike in our Sunday best.
Wilderness church.
Send up a heel-clack prayer.
Screaming marmot
foggy clearing.

Goofy to GQ
you find the gumption
to talk about astrology—
I mean, astronomy.
We discover Sirius
Cygnus X-1
and inquire about
the status of binary stars.

Call the weekend a feat—
Herculean
perhaps Olympic.

VOLUME UP

It's a special sin to listen alone.
The sound of him
like a cartoon character
frantically trying to find
an object
a camp lamp light
in a cornucopia closet
so I could read another
midnight chapter.

The news now
doesn't land the same—
its alarms softened
by the memory
of someone beside me
to bear it with.

Listening to *Making Breakfast.*
Listening to *Wasted on You.*
Listening to you say:
Wait, don't go yet.

Through all the noise
do you hear my buzz?
This silly little fly
~~on your wall?~~
in your ear?

QUIVER

though we differ in our interlineation / let clay pigeons chart the true trajectory / the tea tray is all herbal / caffeine is the morning itself / we play sharks in linen / the way you say I am right / we rewind to 8 a.m. / where I wanted solstice / to be longer / summer's ministry / on the brink of unrest / we sow a slow pace / steady hands / holding bullets / for every bead of innocent sweat / myths are practical / like risky indulgence / we let our hands house each other / in campfire's divination / we tease the momentum / open up to the risk of loss / that beautiful unknowing / of a comprehensive quiver

NATHAN

One year later, here we are.

All rambunctiously ourselves, together.

I was astonished by April & the mutual chance we took—not just on the broccoli cocktail, our puke-green faces smiling at the humor in the beautiful menu of chance.

The stomach butterflies were right. About you. About everything.

Alaska to Washington. Sing to me; the sound of your voice is anything but a *Careless Whisper*.

BREAKFAST JAM

He makes me French toast—
baked in bulk
drizzled in maple syrup
on a slow morning.
Fresh-squeezed
orange-juice jumpstart.
For once,
I taste sweet.
He jumbles around A-minor
as I strum around
a feeling,
minor love.
Woah.
For a minute there
I lost myself—
in sticky tongues
in the music
in a '90s butt-rock ballad.

THE APARTMENT WHERE

the *Sexy Like Spaghetti* cookbook sits on the kitchen counter, opened to a tried-and-true rye bread recipe. Where Tiger Balm rests on the bathroom vanity alongside cottonwood massage oil, the resin remnants on your skin that I touch. Where the flesh-eating carabid beetles reside in the Igloo cooler, cleaning, literally to the bone, your lynx skull that you trapped last winter. Where you lived with another lover, from another lifetime, last year. Where the dust had finally settled, at the doorstep, from her departure. Where you snuck my love in, slowly. Where you welcomed me. Wanted to be my home.

LA POEL, WASHINGTON

Aggravate the lake with our leap-
ing. Simply safe: La Poel. Addicted

to the water vapor in your shower.
The strum in this ebullient

ear. Bedsheet acoustics. Stuck
in July's collateral. Am I

at the seam of summer?
What brain bit makes us

become? Neuroscience
doesn't establish the answer;

it begs the question: Will I be
enough? Extraordinarily

normal? I ask the man who says
yes, and doesn't even have to think

about it. Men are often handy,
but it's the one who best knows

the simplicity of a finger. There.
He says: *The hippocampus*

is named after the seahorse.
But do I form the memories

of us just like the movies?
Re-run, re-peat

until *this* becomes habitual.
Button up that silly armoire

and be anything but pearl
snaps and perfunctory

bliss. I'll tell you
all about Santa Fe.

How I am learning
about the Colorado pine

(trying to forget about all of the
Washington pining). Do we

wean off of or wage war
to end a thing? Divulge

in the blue-green hour
what is kryptonite

and what keeps
us together?

HEADS OR TAILS

Every fluctuation
of a penny

in heads-or-tails orbit
is cosmic decision-making.

Yes-or-no ambiguity
while copper is airborne.

To-do-or-not-to-do
suspension.

An upheaval
of gravity. 50/50

contingency. Dial
each of your digits.

Delete. Disregard
the coin's verdict.

UNRESTRAINED

Alight

alas

we are all the better

for it.

Coexist on your chest

hairs.

The sky is still kind

to second chances

No-shirt

vouchers.

Open-seasame legs.

Temptation folklore.

Coax the door

hinges

to shut.

Candle
admiration.

Courting
intelligence.

Lodge yourself into hand holding.

Rise like
civilizations.

Roar until our defenses

drop.

The closure we find
in curtains.

Restraint
is the rabbit

hole.

I am

no
longer
Alice.

Adrenaline
speed
we go.
Dancing
in
danger's halo.

GENTLE AS THE DRUGS

the dark is
only perfect
when you're here—
psilocybin.
surrender.

clutch the
delicate absence
tell the atoms:
you are irreplaceable.

photobooth.
cheese.

flashes: daggered jolts.
memory lightning wants
to shudder
shutter
shut
the door.
lead me upstairs.
defy
                    being
                                        vertical.

how unfair—
this blouse impatience.
rings don't make us insolvent.
creases in skin
are evening caretakers.

stencil your chest
marksmanship.
imprint.
stamp.
turn off the damn lamp—
our warm aura
is enough
to see
the season
of unmasking.

listen:
fall
equinox.
summer passing
breaking—
faster than knowing freckles.

too tired to pick the banjo?
strum silhouettes instead.
light
as we come.
we only smoke
flowers
when we are
wild &
feral from silk.

QUEEN OF HEARTS

Scar to scale—
it finally secedes
into a sealed wound.

Slip out of what we once
were. Unlevel
the cards. Stack

the night against
alarms. Disassemble
ourselves

into aces. Close
as converging continents
let gravity dictate

the dropping of lace.
Predict the intersection. Gasp
then guess

the number of shivers. Make
the shakes stay. Taste
this salt-lick

skin. Savor
the sound of a bed-
spring. King

cotton. The quiet
horizontal we
achieve.

Abate the
the Monday lateness. Be
with me

like tunnel
vision. We were friends
in fathoms. Now

let the lust lapse
into something
more profound.

MUSIC FESTIVAL NEWS

Crest the concert hill.
Discotheque distractions—
we're in the mushroom zone.
Is it hard to disassociate?
Floral whiff
ganja gargantuan sniff.
I want our limbs to reflect
the skin's localities.

We skip the detours
go straight to deepening.
Directionally delusional
as we bend
all flexible tailgate
truck-bed joints.

Tousled mullets wield
their own strange strength.
Ample horsepower
brunette man(es);
I want to ride
the high
of a wink
your Stetson.
How many kitchen calendars
of you
do I need?
I want the months to pass
in flabbergast.

Guided your hands to my waistline.
Spun 180 degrees
when you called me
Lady Lancee.

Archangel antidote
lead me through crowds
of neon confetti.
Fend off the strobe
bluegrass
bubbles.

Finally equidistant.
Eager for entertainment.
We don't let our lips

wait

to part with
confidence.

But lips
part
with confidence

when they

wait

long

enough.

Read the sensual circular.
Extra! Extra!
You're just in.
Hear the encore—
are we resonating?

Dance with me
in knotted-cherry defiance.

PLUS ONE ABSENCE

Corset me into an updo.
Lackluster eyeliner.
Spoon feed me the vows
I'm wounded
from wanting too much.
Aching for more
than adjournments
and constant social
acclimatization.

Plus-one absences.
Classic conversation.
How do you know the bride?

Pair me with groomsmen
who are all appetites.
Antagonize them
with being single.
Have a couple supple
slow dances to prove a point
about my lack of passion
my lack of *yeehaw*
(despite my two-stepping boots).

Waver with whiskey and Coke.
Rum and mingle
until my glass evaporates.
New beginnings pair
well with the gin.
The tonic
is bouquet-catching irony.

Playlist roulette
and remix with being
in my collegiate city.
Debrief the risk

of oversharing congratulations
and childhood traumas.
Cheers!

I'm all aisle runaway.
Remember me leaving in June?
Last August?
What more can I give you
but a grand quiet exit?

Tonight, will I bear witness
to his glide aftershave?
All smooth talker.
All jawline
and simmered boutonnière.
Will he charge in with a glance?
Backpedal me
into a room
only we are privy to?
Have a nebulous night
with fumbling neckties?
Let my level-headedness lapse
like my astrological downfall?
Jet set away
in his pajamas?

He is cheeky, I concur.
Say *I'm fine*
to the wedding
wing-woman matchmaker
who shuffles me toward
serotonin-boost bachelors.

But how do I tell her that
I stall every time
I detect your skin?
Radiate a smile
when you appear
in a serendipitous radius?

How do I tell her
how much I remember?

From two time zones away
I'll have a tournament in my mind
about right timing
and tessellated ages.
I have been trying
in all my forthrightness
to say *I love you* in my head.
To say *I miss your mullet.*
Your '95 Nissan Hardbody.
I swear it was almost loud enough
for you to hear
3,574 miles away.
Yet here I am
in iris rain.
Laboring to look
good enough
for strangers
for myself even.

What's left: My chardonnay wit
corresponding with suits
and holly hocks
offering up a belated wink
and waltzes
to the willing.

I replay
over and over
how you used to tell me
my blue eyes always
gleamed most
in wedding light.

FIRE STATION 4

I pass by Fire Station 4
on my work commute
where the firemen
play spikeball.
My local firemen
are up to the no-trouble
kind of wholesome.
No fires to tame
that day
until I matched
(ironically on Tinder)
with Ben—
mustached and muscular,
just how you'd expect a firefighter
to look.
Ben happened to be
one of the lunchtime
spikeballers I caught.
Less "fire patrol," more
"keep balls off the ground"
"keep balls in the air." Juggle
almost, a flame, luckily
not a heart, at least. We can stay warm
this fall, see
what Santa Fe has to offer. Jujitsu
me into lockdown, pin me down
because I wanted it, to wrestle
with the grass, to watch
how a man can turn heat
into watercolor, tuck me in
at night, teach me
the art of self-defense, dousing

my angered defiance with a doodle
of a dalmatian, you know, like
firefighter stereotypes? He breaks them
with every corner-booth
can I pay?
Every post-sleepover
breakfast conversation:
How do you like your eggs?
Over hard?
Let's make this
easy. Does it
have to be
Taylor Swift
Red? Destiny
be damned, I'll always
do it
for the poem. For the gut-
punch feeling. Who cares
if it is fleeting? Flames.
Heat-lightning heart.
I'll be burgundy lace, learn
how to twist a cherry stem, siren the Syrah,
receive bouquets a-bounty, pop the merlot
for a pomp-and-circumstance sip, sangria
candy, stumble on sidewalk,
have him be my crimson
bandaid, blush uncontrollably, sober
up in our scarlet sheets,
maybe dream
of garnet's blaze
and be enraptured
by an inferno of rubies.

LEAVING THE FRIEND ZONE AT THE MUSIC FESTIVAL

Let Friday morning seep in—
that stroll to the quiet side of serendipity.

Be my surprise campsite visitor.
I didn't know you'd be here, but

moments braid us
into familiar places:

music festivals
my rainbow jumpsuit body

desire—
all things patiently delayed.

Effect affecting me
for mullet youth

and psychedelic shirts
that would be unbuttoned

by Saturday.
Press pause—

just before the melodic intersection
of tongues.

Do we take this
where we wish

or where
we should?

Sometimes it takes years
to finally speak

freely—
less fumbling

of lips.
Acid remarks remake us

kingly, dipping
making bets on the best band.

Please—I mean
if you want—

stay
for this tailgate banter

breakfast.
Ooo at my glitter eyes.

I apologize
for your four-year yearning.

But I didn't know how to
flip energy

until EDM
and electricity.

When I finally left
the friend zone

I grabbed your hand
like a free beer—

greedy
drunk.

Waistline reverb
coaxing the bass-drop.

The kissing and missing
turned kinetic.

I fly, standby
still unsure.

Yes, I saw
the *I like bushy beavers*

bumper sticker. I get it now.
I know why I couldn't write off

the interlude.
Call me

unexpectedly spicy
then send me southbound.

I let the West wear me
like wanting. You—

I can't regret what leaves me
whetted—

that whirlwind weekend.
All I can say

as I leave
is something

not memorable:
Don't change your name

but if you did
I'd call you *Ziggy*.

Keep my avocado plant alive
in Alaska

for as long as you can
(even if I don't expect it);

and maybe we don't wait
another four years

again.

RETURNING

Tuck and roll into another
month. Habits are attractive
like snow-
men. The dream state
is knowing I'll come back
eventually.

November has a crunch, and I don't mean the dismembered leaves. There's a habitual need to hermit. The post-Halloween jitters hackle my back. My ability to light a match careens. Tinder is useless (not just the dating kind). Experiment with the seasons. Call upon the dusty grimoire. Ask a witch the first lesson in issuing a spell. There's laws governing attraction, but what rules dictate the interference of magic? My fingers are feverish for December. For reconvening with dreams. Nightfall does a tuck and roll as I rebuild snowmen. We all feel the jeopardy of sun. Catch my text message at an improbable moment. Wishing I'd come back. Wishing I'd never left at such an inopportune time.

November's crunch &
hermiting attraction.
My jitters light a match
search the grimoire
for a love spell.
Fever-dream memory melts
snowmen interactions.
The sun and I play jeopardy.
What is as inopportune
as saying:
I wish you were here.
Roll, then tuck.
Habits return
as dismembered magic.

FISHBOWL

I want the consensus
of mutual eye-peeps.
Wardrobes reveal subtle
tattoos, ties,
suited glances.
Rifle through
my airspace. Cubicle
circles, square desks
surround us—
herded perimeters. Parameters
of a tumbling pencil
and the workday innuendo
as we are separated by glass.
Alternative versions of us
are visceral. Route-seeker
around Saturn, fire-destroy
planetary wants. Take over
nostalgia. Waterboard the best
memory. Unlearn the touch
that undid buttons
that made buttermilk pancakes. Pester
the pillows for more hushed
closure.
I am nervous
to re-orbit others—parse
my individualism from my nature
to collide. Revitalize
my looking your way.
Rewind it, over and over,
turtle-speed. Follow
the ridges of impressionable
skin. Surmount a palm
and undergo breath's
escapement. Assume
the embarking will be
transformative, and the bliss

of returning to familiar tectonics
will be the surrender
of a lifetime.
Wake
to a billion universes
that keep you on this track—
telling time is a lie's escapement.
The truth
of leaking tears
is regeneration's secret. Knock
on the window pane. Wave.
Whirlwind
surprise—this, this.
Foundationally
I yearn for waxing
and waning seasons,
music. The banjo,
soundtrack pluck, self-evident
caminos. Rhododendron
casino. Jackpot
garden party. Teacup
symphonies. Appeals—
your agency
across the way
is wonderland. For all
my detail orientedness
I love overhangs
and abstracts. I like a piecemeal
drink and never-ending
stories, a stanza
so fresh my tongue
is all coffee juice
and juxtaposed
taste. You. Caffeine.
In the dead of winter, I dress
like spring, bike
like a crayon, visibly
rainbow. Blush. Aura
of slow pedals. Professionally spin,

sink into actuality
keyboards
office aquariums.
Acquire waterlogged hope.
Keep my head above
desire, deadlines. Eagerly
swim to the nearest exit.

n. deep sorrow, grief, or regret for something, often expressed through words or actions; an elegiac melody in writing

read receipts
ruin relationships

LICK JESUS; BOMB SUPERMAN

I want homemade ice cream. To hear Baltimore blues in cigarette ambiance. I want to be a sellout. Stagecoach energy rattling my bones. I sit thinking of the shrewd judgment of pennies, personhood. I get the "ick" when nails scratch the chalkboard, but I only shiver when the chimes call him home. I want to be number one at something—anything. The best at lounging in the shade, centuries of sunburnt shoulders. *Atta girl*, I want to say to myself, for achieving almost nothing: a life next to rocks and water. Six pounds of séance lighter, a strip-tease medium between flesh and guy. I want sativa saliva, stiletto fangs, and French martini daydreams. The habit of mouthing your name across the bar, a fifty-foot whisper whiplash on my tongue. I want to quit thinking: *Who would Jesus bomb today*? Superman in a waffle cone? Catwoman? Cookie-dough countries? The damn boy that broke my heart?

SPOOK

Fickle guytrash, coming
only at night.
Gossamer moon man
anomalies made flesh—
ghastly in the plural.

Ghoul gunpowder
shot-down threats
of an October orgy.

Spook!
Mistook his mask
for heart massacre.
Hazardous skull skills—
to be the devil
incarnate
is a full-time profession.

FISHING FOR SMELTS ON KANAKANAK BEACH

Slow-motion mornings—
the trudge
the delayed boot-sink.

The ground hardens
then softens
when September remembers
itself.

My phone still dials
your number.
Muscle memory.
Accidental cause.

Indecent space folds in—
we made the most
of the mesh
while it lasted.

After calm
there's still storm.
The ocean always
corrects. Conversation
tide. Tsunami talk.

We're fishers.
Fiends.
Friends, even.
Dinner is a fresh catch.
The outgoing current
is the only truth—
taking us away with it.
Five smelts still
gleaming in our net.

THRUSH'S SONG

Into the thickets—
throaty thoughts eject.
Thorax confession.

Remember that time
we tossed out *I love you*?

But, when you hum a tune
too often
you stress the song out
the more you sing it.

FOR SURE

I don't know what it means
to be certain
about anything.

Right now, all I feel
is m i d
a i
r
suspension—
below me:
glaciers
disappearing
(maybe lovers, too).

The height of an exodus comes
after a genesis.
I'm somewhere
in the | middle | now.

Last August
I wore a white dress
to a friend's murder mystery party.
He said: *You should wear that to a wedding.*
I thought he meant someone else's.
(He meant ours).
I shook my head in denial—
improper (almost) matrimony etiquette.
He was already picturing us
aisle-bound.

He offered me free courses
in Wrench-onomics 101—
a tool torque tutelage.
Newton meters to foot-pounds.
Six quarts of 0W-20 Mobil oil.
Hand me the 1/16, please.

He voluntarily unclogged
the shower drain
grilled ribs for my parents
the first night they came to visit me
in my new apartment
on Nelson Ave.

But, can I be sure
that *this* is love?

Will I be sure
when he asks me to marry him?

Will I be sure
the sun will rise tomorrow?

That I'll open my eyes?

When will I be sure?

When I spot the ocean
I'm bombarded with our trip
to the Cape.
How I found my first ukidama—
a glass ball Japanese fishermen used
to keep their nets afloat—
then my fifteenth.
How thrilling novelty is
(until it isn't).

I'm in the bleak moment
after your rose-colored affair.
When the uncertainty seeps in
like a crackling log
giving in to fire.

Will I ever be sure
when he tells me the messages
from his ex mean nothing?

Will I ever be sure
when he keeps looking
at other women?

Never.

Until I finally am.

ARTIFACTS OF ANOTHER WOMAN

Relics, really.
Nebulous associations.
Lapsed gauges of gratification—
every cell in her still yearns.
Strings to her.
Bullets to me.

To "pine after"
is an affair
fit for a forty-something prowl.
Hunt a memory—
not me.
Daisies don't know
the difference
between sun and shade;
they just want
the right type of tending.
Oh, gentle gardener
you've dug quite
the ditch.

A synopsis of amendments
accusations
and the aftermath.
The math-ematician
mortician
muse—
perfectly calculated endings
nonetheless.

What do we bind ourselves to?
Rock?
Rugged man?
The assumption of reality
is a falsity
warped into halved truth.

Mirages mesmerize.
But why am I always
left questioning
the validity
of chemistry?

Vacillate.
Renege.
Offer an answer
as amorphous as truth
for just one more ounce
of bedsheet.

Dial a sorry.
Play Romeo.
Drink the vial—
alone.

A *yes*
is a loose interpretation
of a *no*.

Sorry:
a wavering pledge.
A wedge
driven deep
by young-fooled destinies.

Holding on:
delinquent rapture.
Recklessness knows me
better than I know myself.

Scratch the surface
then take me
down
for
one

last
regret.

Irises—
insignificant
insufficient
insufferable.

Brown-eye disguises
confide under
cower behind
collapse in my arms
and calls it *commitment*.

Revel in me
like reconciliation
before my revelation.

Another ring.
Telephonic memory.

Now we both know
who it is,
who *she* is.
So why—
why are you still
so desperate
to answer?

AT ARM'S LENGTH

Do you love me the way you want a hiccup to go away? To be temporarily breathless. Why do you love me in the way you always choose secondary colors? Is it too much to ask you to love expressly? Or am I just a behind-the-scenes Broadway understudy? You are loving me satellite-orbiting-earth close, which is to say, from afar.

IF ONLY

I could name this
an absurdity, a one-off

interrogation.
I love you

echoes
from a bond before me.

Exhume your ego
while I draw The Fool—

then fall

without

catchment.

Your *sorry*:
requiem.

Goodbye—
diaphragmatic.

With every evening
exhale

There
is
no
antithetical

liberation.

I DON'T KNOW

if loons ever feel
like lunatics.

I don't know
why breakups feel
like
drug withdrawal.

I don't know why
fireflies
illuminate.
I don't know why he kept
Emily, a Snapchat
secret, like his

flesh-eating
beetles.

I don't know if otters
cheat on a mate.
Do wild horses
know
they are
free
to
roam?

AFTERMATH

Choke on thick smoke—
the inhalation of a transitory month.
What is failure but a flippant curse?
We twine ourselves into compromise
become a budding relapse—
slow downturns.

It's too late for lyricism
too late for love—
clearly we're crumbling
under the weight of clothes.

Resurrect the sex
some semblance of union.
Prisoners to a light left on.

Your open-door policies
press me closer.
I'm upright—
a still-standing stutterer
kissing pavement:
begging
for bloody-knee reciprocity.

Tourniquet solutions
for what can't coagulate—
crimson lies.
Yield truth
like a lance.
Trounced by the aftermath
of an alternative ending.

Arm.
Man.
Get.
Down.

Acclimate to being alone.
Let dreams—
like you—become
all the more
amorphous.

CHEATING

Call it timing.

Call it:
She's just a friend
I forgot to tell you about.
(And forgot to tell
my last girlfriend about, too).
Is she a slip-your-mind slut?

Call it:
I sent her my homemade canned salmon.

Call it:
It's fine that she texts me every Valentine's Day.

Say:
Is it not okay if women find me appealing?

Say:
How can I make you less jealous of other women?

Call it:
I'm not a bad person.

I'll call it:
True character.

I'll call it
off
when you call it
anything
other than what it
is.

CLEAN SLATE

Farewell—exodus out of his mouth:
no take-backs.
Return is beyond salvage.
Calm, old-country static—
the symphony of a suburban outlaw.
Spring arrives, and he departs;
the sun rises over west Abilene.

The making of a man goes something like this:
forged by freedom and love
whether he likes it or not.

At the bar, in a swell of Marlboro fog
he'd taken her hand,
slipped a metal lasso 'round her finger.
Diamond promises
were hard to keep—
easier to walk away from
a dead-end dirt road decision.

The past now lies fallow in the farm's pasture.
On Easter, she hangs her wedding gown
freshly laundered, on the clothesline
with dust-bowl delusions
that he'll return.

The thought of flight
and fresh starts
enters Texas.
The wind finally bellows
whipping the fabric—
and her—
free.

LEDA AND THE SWAN

– *after William Butler Yeats*

Mere myth or mortal—
can a swan's gaze captivate?

A daze: impermissible seduction.
Strange shapeshift—
plumage doth flock

to something fair
something airy.

Her flesh, plundered.
Her breast, fleeting.
Lineage born—
adultery by godly desire.

Sparta labors twofold
reckoning with aggressive conception.

Within her: nested indecency.
She—
a Greek hatchery.

TO THE TRAPPER

who has caught
a new scent. I see you

wait

patiently.

Your insecurity–
palpable

at her pulse

at her
brown locks

at her
fawning

her
frailty.

You wait.

Wait.

Wait.

I go
while

you

keep

pursuing.

What am I missing
from the rom-coms?
Toothpick affairs?
The sex scene?
All breasts
bed frames
we ramshackle
against.
Lick my clit—
this closing-leg envelope.

Eleventh-hour forgiveness
I feign.
Skip the butterflies
go straight
to the goosebumps.
Fishtail
to the credits
Your name.
The end.

And still—
I can't say
I didn't predict
when your tongue
went rogue
on another woman's
rouged lips.

LOVE IS THE PART WE ~~PLAY~~ PRAY

Love
is a parting
prayer.

Love is
parting.

Love is prayer.

Love is part
prayer.

Love is the prayer
that we part.

I THINK I COULD HAVE HATED YOU IF

you hadn't told me how
in college
you felt ashamed
of your small-town education—
how you couldn't read or write
as well as the others
how every essay
was an embarrassment.

the curse of cursive
recursive beliefs
fumbling nouns.

when you first met me
I confessed
I wanted to be a writer.
you gave me
an engraved wooden pen.

now
in my hands
the book
you inspired me to write.

your hands—
elsewhere.

HALCYON

Lovers are drawn
to pure
lodestone.
Metallic smiles
streaks of lust—
lightning theory.

Hurricane-eye calm.
He makes earthen promises.
sings *la la lune* tunes
remaking June
into platitudes.

Summer clambers over
midnight's thread
heady for lapsed halcyon.

Jagged bolts
revolt into
horizontal polarization.

The moon lends me starlight
sentimental over being
quartered—
lunar fragmentation.

Loss of eternity's extremity.
Loss of self.
Eclipsing binary.

PROTAGONIST

Maybe the months become oval-shaped—
like the splintered presence
of this invited party guest
slipping out through the backdoor.

Blame it on Irish descent:
my habit of unplanned exits
excusing myself from moments
excluding my narrative
from the night.

When I saw you with her
my eyes watered against my will.
I guess I don't mingle well
with puncture wounds.

The memory of us
is an unseen force.

Time is trying me
harder than it ever has.
Why am I always tethered
to every tired trope?

God
how hard it is
to be the protagonist?

Can I cut to the fairytale?
It's supposed to be happy
right?

BUT IT WAS A SMALL TOWN

He was 42, I was 28.
But the town was small.

He had a habit of looking back—
blondes, brunettes—
watching, lingering.
But the town was small.

He still spoke to his ex
(make that exes).
One from twenty years ago
another from just two.
But the town was small.

He said he was clean.
I had a pulse
when it all began.
But the town was small.

He gave me flowers
gadgets, trinkets—
this-that things.
Illusions, all of them.
But the town was small.

When I left
the world was vast.

COMMONPLACE

is just where we hang out now.
These gray hairs?
They make me a fox.

So get your fix—
for a moment.
Let's mold our bodies
into something plural.

Come with. *Boom.*
Grenade or Grenada.
First class.

Honey
I like your sass.
Asshole?
That's not me.

Trust.
Hold my hand.
I think I . . .
like you . . .

Love?
I'm not sure.
I like the chase.
Hunting guide by trade.

Plenty of fish—
I catch, reel.
So real.
Bait. Hook.
It's simple logic:
I like tails.
And texts
(from my ex).

Wait—
where were we?

Sex.
Next.

Now:
me
and you,
(and her).

That's what I choose—
for now.

Forever (maybe)
if you keep
believing
every word
I say.

TAKE WHAT YOU WANT

now *that*'s what I call a lukewarm kiss—
not the hurricane kind.
just the edge of shrapnel
that misses the mark.

i'm an apparatus for experimentation
minimizing shivers
between conduction
making parting
past-tense.

trust is a fallow winter.
each flake
desperate separation
that knocks us off-center
in the midst of dreamt perpetuity.

everything is true *and* false—
to falter
to flirt
to frame me
in the backslashes
of your newest infatuation.

forgiveness
is just negotiation.

dedication and deceit
are hand-me-down patterns
he acquired.

Right before the gaslight
he'd preach:
Good people deserve good things.

BLOOD MOON

Pick me clean
pick me last.
There's sinew in the sky
come midnight.

What if I don't
love you to the moon
and back?
To the Earth
and back?
To your place
back to mine?

There's no formula
for second place.
To be the girl
who's a forgotten leaflet
left to peruse empty spaces.

Bit by mosquito lust.
Under the umbra
I swear
falsely.
To diatribes.
To deliverance.

To that which outweighs
a stream.

It's a high payment
to be reactive.

You say I rush over boulders
then brag that she's all ballet.

The hallway where we first kissed
is a bitter ratio.
Microphone quiet
where I sit
alone
yet under the same atmospheric creed.

On this side of town
you wouldn't know it
but shadows lie more
than a forged love letter.

Signed:
Yours ~~Truly~~ Temporarily.

KNUCKLE VELVET

Let this be my double-door exit.
Call it dramatic.
Call it disgruntled.
The want to towel-throw
for no reason.

I'll knuckle my way out
wanting to claw back
to the beginning.
The before.

He held me at shotgun's length.
Coerced me to be calm
when all I felt was calamity.

I'll be brutish.
Let you backhand me
with a compliment.
Be belligerent
with an *I love you.*
Banter with the idea
of anniversaries.

The fall from undressing
is risqué.
The uplift of a veil
without a proper introduction
can be fate.
Incense them with touch
before we enter the causeway.

The induction
of the wound
you imparted
wasn't my prediction;
but a delicate premonition
can destroy us before
the intermission.

We're at the part-or-mold intersection.

Confuse this heart's contusion.

Derail another lover
to purgatory.

The joints of my left finger
don't resist
enclosure
as much as they have been
taught to.

For some reason
I don't doubt
the poetic vows.

I trust the nature of velvet
but only how it felt
to me back then.

OVER, DONE

no-apology appetizer—
femme-fatale penne
male-dominated dessert.

house-wine confession
rare-steak truths spilled
across napkins
knife-serrated shock
tip-over-kettle rage.

fork-in-the-road romance
table chaos
cutlery ends.

HAY SCAR

Tie the bandana around
my neck
and let
nostalgia suffocate
us.

There's an indecipherable
intolerance to distance—

eyes are golden
morphology—

the storytelling
of wrinkles

the instruction
of a gentle
wind.

I recant
the wanting.

Simple chores
make us
clean
again.

The drainage of a sink
full of dirty dishes.
Scratched porcelain.
Chipped china

aches
to mouth
our old clinking
conversations.

The hay scars
on
my
forearms—

you said they were
harmless

but never told me
a long sleeve
could save.
Amongst an acre,
we could feel
infinite.

But infinity
is a sacrificial lure:
bobber
head
glassy lake.
The last
of which I could take

of it
all.

Of the other
women.
Of the man you
pretended to be.

Of the havoc you wreaked

out of habit.

Now, I skip

over

the flyover

states.

Avoidant of farmland
p u l s e s.

I'd trade September for August

or November

anytime—
anytime
to forget
the sins
the tomatoes
and the garden
squash

squandered away.

Skip the single-cab
closeness.

Driving-off-into-the-distance
ghosting

is hallowed. Howling
on interstate
pavement.

There's reverence
in finality, saying:

Don't limit me
to boulders
silver—
or cities you swore
I'd never make it in

without you.

APARTMENT STILL LIFE

The front door mat catches
remnants of outside:
gravel, a leaf, snow—
sometimes, a lost key.

The space—400 square feet—
cupboards full of mismatched mugs
twenty-five cents apiece.
Purple plates.
A mecca of mason jars.

My attempt at nesting.
An attempt to ground,
though bound to a second story.

Stories: some planned
some unexpected.
Some hopeful.
Some stuck in their climax.
Some that don't want to be turned on—
like the unplugged television.

Static, preempted.
Winter brings new stalemates.

The spider plants inch
toward what's left of the light.

There used to be sincerity
and warmth
in my bed sheets—flannel.
A fridge stocked with nourishment.
Two toothbrushes in the bathroom.
A body beside mine.

Now the windows beg
for new vantage.

That's the crux of the couch—
trying to get off it.
Giving myself permission
to live any yearning alternative.

Or none of them.

Or just this.

Sometimes, I picture myself
walking past the front door mat
fracturing the lock
leaving this life entirely.

Him, too.

FORTRESS

I've put too many men
behind bulwarks—
isolation at its finest.

Mote defense.
No time for ingress
no space for egress.

Regrets?
That's another matter
entirely.

Too trenchant.
Forgetting—
a more appreciable act.

There are teary palpabilities.
Irascible onlookers
long for something:

Anger.
Amelioration.
One and the same.

I remain afar.
Afraid.

I take on air.
My lungs—
the quietest breathing apparatus.

ROMEO

Kiss me, kill me
with love. For it is
utter antidote
and utter poison.

KALMIA POLIFOLIA

Pale-laurel face.
We offer a chance
to this terminal cluster.

Found in southern Minnesota—
lost on me.

The leaves come in pairs.
Imagine that.

BREAKING UP OVER THE PHONE

Not the ideal
situation. Desperation. Done.
Hello.
Cherry-on-top time bomb.
Impetus: Miscommunication.
Mistrust: On full display.
A tip: Don't talk to your ex.
It's an appalling atrocity.
Yet I am loving
goodbye's dial tone.

CURSE YOU

Forget the poems
that read like curses—
like ouija-board omens
we summoned at night.

Lower me into a dug-out grave—
a bitter fall.
I fancy something
like open-casket honesty.

Honestly
I'm most myself
when I'm asleep and auburn-cheeked
like October hounding your front porch.

Please, uncover hell—
then bring me
the friend I've made
of forgiveness.

Oh, call me crazy
loving your pitfalls
pitying you
then pitching a fit
like a pumpkin.

Patch up my cold feet.
Tell the stars:
tone it down a notch—
so I don't get too hopeful
like a twenty-something girl
spiraling into happenstance
and shaky-kneed reneging.

How irrelevant I am
to trust deep-venom touching.

Press me
against your estranged chest
like it's the warmest thing
I'll find all fall.

EARSHOT

stomach full of Martinelli's
swallow the echoes
of empty park benches
kiss frozen street posts—
this is the New Year's Eve stuck-ness
I feel.
there's steel on my tongue
an efflux of sickness.

I'd say my heart
is just an extension
of my ability to be yours.

shhh.
I spill secrets
like I do to red lights.
it's to stop.
remember?
my lover, lost in 2024.

screaming is easy satisfaction—
starting anew is askew
in the snow.
hitting reset
is a faulty button
.

tonight, I dance
with shimmering-eyeshadow deities,
disclose to the DJ
our first-dance song,
fall apart
on 5th Avenue.
I wish this were a figment,
a left-finger ring
glinting in the strobe light.

forever was an easy hill
to die on—
even though
you never meant
to prove it.

3... 2... 1...
another countdown
I'm supposed to celebrate.
circumvent the drawstring confetti
the whippersnappers—
POP. POP. POP.
was the last sound
you heard.

FIRST FALLEN LEAF

Inhale
the impending thunderstorm.

Northeast sighs—
still nostalgic for summer.

Polar pomegranate seltzer:
a poem
a plus-one.

I'm in a flash—
back to Vermont.

Rolling-hill twenties
coming to a close.

Buying the goddamn
maple leaf Christmas ornament
for the hypothetical tree
I'll share with
a hypothetical boyfriend
come not-so-hypothetical December.

It's fragile—
these months we move through
each one holding a holiday
like a wedding date.

The Green State
whispers *change is coming.*

Autumn never leaves
anything upturned
(unless it already was).

EARTH, WIND, FIRE.

Elemental September.
Approach love like a dance floor—
no rules.
Let loose.
Absorb disco.

There's an ensemble of trees
as limbs. Will we circle
the forest forever?

As rehearsed
we vow.

Wow. The sky offers
an eyedropper evening—wet
window-gazed.
Hand me a glass.
A champ. No pain.
In my chest
I believe in libations
but sober spills my secrets.

It's surreal
to be prompted by a heart
to echo an *I do*
to sit in the aisle
and hold my peace.
No fatherly blessing.
No shotgun swell.

Corsets are a crime
and I committed bride-ry.
Left-finger trust.

Tell me—
(rings aside)—

do diamonds ever shatter?

IN FLUX

Uncharted territory.
What is tolerable
and what is transgression?
The answer is gray—
the blur of believing
in being held
without restraint.

This time
it's requited
required.
But are we free
if we tether?

You only feel contrite
when you don't communicate.
Feet tuned to flight.
Hands trained
against affixation.
Wounds open
only in secrecy.

Weather in flux.
A compass—
never a dictator.
The water rises
by torrent.
The current is our guide.
Dear,
when is high tide?

Is this it?

NO MORE MEDDLING WITH MUSES

Realizing what we can
and cannot meddle in.
Caring is conveyed
in short distances.

Is salvation the salve between our beings?
It takes bull-in-china-shop rage
to walk away quietly. Forever
is something salient.

Numb us with tincture and touch
until rain radiates a fruitful cleanse.
Cozy up to the weather—
don't wait for its moody passage.

When will the muse
ever have meaning
again?

Droplet of a tailgate
I'll sit beneath the torrent.
It is the monsoon sanctuary—
an umbrella urge.
Puddle my ink.
Plunge into a poem, headfirst—
it's what I know best.

DON'T GET ME THE DIAMOND

Diamonds are forever.
Really?
It can feel contrived—to collapse
into each other
to pour our passion into
ovals and ownership.

Smoke-ring promises are hard to hold.
Poised to last, they say.
But relationships break
even when the gemmed band doesn't.

So say what it's worth.
Possession
Prize.
To unionize—surely.
Love has a lustre
that gleams, at first
then dulls
when mined carelessly.

Vow me something softer.
Vow me this:
a poem.
Vow me opal, moonstone
amber, pearl—
things prone to damage
yet choosing to be
soft anyway.

NO TRACTION

in that Patsy Cline song
knocking on your door—
crazy downpour kind of love.
The soggy afterthought.

Remember? Fish-head soup?
The way you broke my heart
then boiled it for comfort?
Served me the same dish
over and over.

Late-night knocking
became our reconciliation loop.
That damn knocking.

Hi, he'd say.
I'm still here.
I'm sorry.

Slip into my body.
Expel the intrusion.
But forgiveness—
it's less olive branch
more muddy tire.
It spins. It sinks.
It's nimble in the worst ways
always dragging us deeper;
has the tendency to keep us
stuck.

PARTED

The ghost of the willow dances
amongst your floral sheets.
The ache of your banjo
holds more than mournful strings.

Indecsion haunts you
down every river bend.
Thumb through an old picture
just for one more stolen glance.

Every minute you wait
thistle takes another stab.
There's promise in the poison
and lethalness in the land gap.

Defiant as you hope,
chords outlast regret.
Entrapped by an almost forever
in a longing, lingering fret.

Disdain the distance
and all her lapsing miles.
Our bones carry us through
every avoided marriage aisle.

Held by rope now
like it's your last golden plea.
We are merely fools
parted by states of being
immeasurable rock
& sea.

FOR, IN THE RARE EVENT, IT IS LOVE

A WEDDING POEM

Does one fall in love
with or in Vermont?
Only the fortunate do both
and run away to Alaska
anchoring on W. 83rd.

That Dillingham date in July
a mountain, a moment—
green as an emerald summer:
Fate is foolproof for the few
with O'Brien Irish luck.

This love between two hearts
is not just a legality
but a king salmon catch
a lifetime Darn Tough sock warranty
a gentle Gregory Alan Isakov song.

Most of all
it's an admit-two ticket
standing front and center
of the wedding aisle.
A union
an encore
a state of becoming
the *Means*
to their shared ending.

ABOUT THE AUTHOR

Lancee Whetman is a lover, a lust-er, and a woman frequently caught in the looping ache between wanting and being wanted. Her work lives in that fevered space between blush and becoming exclusive. She writes with the pulse of someone who is all butterflies, then all heartbreak, all too often. Her collections include: *Blinded by Feeling* (2023), *Further West & Fireweed* (2024), *Chapped Lips* (2025), and *Rosy-Cheeked* (2026).

ABOUT THE BOOK

I like you, like you borrows its title from Lancee's favorite 2009 film, *Cloudy with a Chance of Meatballs*—a story about an earnest inventor, Flint Lockwood, who creates a machine that turns water into food, and an aspiring weather reporter, Sam Sparks.

What begins as a miraculous technological wonder quickly spirals into chaos, raining cheeseburgers and spaghetti across their small island town, Swallow Falls. Flint and Sam join forces to save not only the town but the world itself. In the end, amidst fighter-jet pizza slices, raging gummy bears, and peanut-brittle allergies, it's the small, perfect confession between them that inspired this collection:

Sam Sparks: Look, I like you, okay?

Flint Lockwood: Like...as a friend?

Sam Sparks: No, I mean "like you" like you.

Flint Lockwood: Me too. I mean, about you.

ACKNOWLEDGEMENTS

What's more than liking your significant other, partner, the person you are dating? Liking your book-assembly team! Cheers and platonic kisses to my beta readers and editors, Zachary Olson, Dave Biegel, and Danica Cotov, as well as my formatter, Kristina Konstantinova. I like y'all!

www.ingramcontent.com/pod-product-compliance
Lightning Source LLC
LaVergne TN
LVHW060501090626
840787LV00040B/686

9798989730230